# Divorce Struggles?

Don Barnes

Published by Don Barnes, 2024.

This publication provides the Author's opinion and neither the publisher nor the author intends to render legal, accounting, or other professional advice with this publication.
The publisher and the author disclaim any personal liability, loss or risk incurred as a consequence of the use and application, directly or indirectly, of advice, information or methods presented in this publication.
First Edition

# Copyright © 2025

# By Don Barnes / Tryune Works!

TRYUNE WORKS! and Life works in threes are trademarks and copyrights of Don Barnes and Tryune Works!

 **LifeWorksInThrees.com**

# Table of Contents

# About the Author

Don is the founder and author of Life Works in Threes!™ E-books. He is a lifelong Texan who has traveled extensively while taking a keen interest in human behavior. His curiosity about life and what drives humans led him to the discovery of how life works in threes. He coined this term as the *Tryune Concept.*

Don attended college on an athletic scholarship and then embarked on a 30-year career in the oil and gas industry. Since the year 2000, he has been a consultant for distributors and manufacturers of various industries. Along the way, he worked on his Tryune discovery in hopes of someday sharing his findings with those struggling unnecessarily... in life. What Don surmised from 40+ years of R&D was that people were struggling unnecessarily because they were not aware that "life works in threes." They, for the most part, have been living their lives <u>by chance</u> rather than<u> by choice,</u> he also discovered.

From this, he began focusing on the "mechanics of life" which shows formulas for success with subjects such as *life, health, money, purpose and so forth.* When people are able to grasp the Tryune Concept, they can apply the formulas with topics that interest them and begin eliminating the struggle. This epiphany is what triggered his Tryune venture and is now on the path of sharing with all who desire to improve on their lives.

Don currently resides in Southern California and Texas while overseeing his businesses and investments.

## Life Works in Threes™

When I was a kid growing up, no one sat me down and said, "Okay Don, I'm going to show you how life works so that you can navigate your way through adulthood." I graduated from school, got married and went about my way with the "learn as you go" concept. It was kind of like putting together a backyard swing set without a set of instructions. Lots of frustration and do-overs, for sure!

My discovery of the "triune" word and noticing how things come together in threes is really what set me off on researching that maybe "life comes in three" ...sort of a mechanical approach to managing life, if you will. I combed the libraries and bookstores for information on this and found one book on the subject that was written back in 1951. The author's name was John S. Arant.

What Mr. Arant had to say is this "For lack of a better name, I have called this *The Triangle of Triumph* and therefore, consistent with the name, since most of these conclusions are built on the geometric figure of the triangle." He continued "All Life and all lives are seated in, and circumscribed by, the triangle. The Author and Source and Director of all life is Himself triune in character – Father, Son, and Holy Spirit. Man is of triple nature – body, mind, and spirit – and within those three there are many triangles – desires, development, decay; intellect, will, sensibilities. Of this "paced interlude in the midst of eternity" which we call time there is the triangle of Past, Present, and Future. Space – that limitless and measureless element of the physical universe – is best known in terms of Height, Breadth, and Depth. Try building yourself some triangles along the lines of your Will, your Work, your Way – You will find some interesting angles.

So, for the first time, I realized that life is designed in a mechanical way to come in threes. That means you don't have to rely on wishing and hoping things turn out okay. You can actually look at the three parts that a particular thing is made of and then apply them to get what you're wanting. Like a three-ingredient recipe or a combination lock. With a combination lock, you need the three exact numbers to unlock the lock...otherwise you will continue to struggle.

Some 40 years later, I accumulated things that work in threes and that's when I knew I needed to share this with anyone wanting answers. To have success/harmony in your life, just apply the three parts of an area you're working on, and things will fall into place. I also learned that the_recipe for success _with just about anything is by doing these three things, consistently – THINK positively, SPEAK positively and ACT positively. For example, if I want to be a successful artist. I would think to myself "I can do this because I have the talent." Then I would speak it this way "Yes, I am working on my art degree and plan to do portraits professionally." Finally, I would act on that by taking art classes and continue crafting my skill. Eventually, I will see the positive results/success I'm looking for.

Conversely, if I think positively but speak negatively...it will cancel out. Or if I speak positively but have no positive action going on...nothing will happen.

I looked up "How Life Works" and "The Mechanics of Life" and these are really talking about the biology of how our cells work and other chemistry. TRYUNE WORKS! teaches that life is kind of like building blocks. Pick a topic you may be struggling with. See the three parts that topic consists of and then start applying them...on a consistent basis. That will help you overcome the struggle and get you back in harmony/success with how life works.

For 30+ years I was a golf instructor (by accident). My two kids had some success playing junior golf and so friends and neighbors would ask me to show them and their kids how to play golf successfully. From all of this, I got pretty good at watching golfers on the driving range and could spot right away why they were struggling with hitting bad golf shots. I was able to do that because I knew the three steps to hitting good golf shots. I learned them from studying golf and played for several decades. I "broke the code" for me so to speak.

So now you know that life works in threes. You can live your life *by choice* rather than *by chance* and that my friend... is the key to a fulfilling life.

**My sanctuary on the Pacific coast**

# Introduction

Navigating life after a divorce can be like stepping into a whole new world, filled with its own set of joys and challenges. One of the biggest hurdles is finding your footing again. Suddenly, you might be faced with decisions you used to make together, like finances or parenting, all on your own. It can feel overwhelming at first, but remember, you're not alone on this journey. Many people have successfully rebuilt their lives after divorce, finding strength they didn't know they had.

Another challenge is adjusting to a new routine. From daily schedules to weekend plans, everything might need a bit of reshuffling. This can be disorienting initially, especially if you were used to a certain rhythm with your ex-partner. But think of it as an opportunity to rediscover what makes you happy and fulfilled. Maybe you'll take up a new hobby, reconnect with old friends, or explore interests you didn't have time for before. Embracing change can lead to unexpected moments of growth and self-discovery.

Emotionally, it's a rollercoaster ride. There may be days when you feel liberated and optimistic about the future, and others when loneliness or regret creep in. It's okay to feel a range of emotions; healing takes time. Surround yourself with supportive friends and family who understand that healing is not linear. Self-care becomes crucial during this time—whether it's through therapy, exercise, or simply taking time to do things that bring you peace. Remember, every day is a step forward, even if it doesn't always feel that way.

# My discovery of the Tryune Concept

Before we dive into divorce struggles and how to overcome them, let me share my discovery of the Tryune Concept and how life works in threes. It all began in the summer of 1982.

I grew up with parents who treated everyone with decency and respect. My three older sisters and I were raised in a home that was "middle-class traditional." We lived in modest homes in different small towns, attended school and church on a regular basis and celebrated all the traditional holidays. Eventually we settled during the spring of 1964 in the big city of Houston, Texas. I'll never forget the vastness of the city and hearing sirens from police cars, fire trucks and ambulances on a regular basis. I was excited and scared at the same time.

Once settled in this fast-paced city, I finished my growing-up years with an academic diploma and sweetheart intact. I got a job, bought a car, got married, bought a house and produced two beautiful babies in a span of about 5 years. Talk about having to grow up fast!

Things went from great in my childhood to absolute misery in my young adulthood. I began to struggle with my job because deep down I just hated what I was doing. This problem created a snowball effect because soon after, my weight, my finances, my relationships, my happiness and everything else worth saving was going down the drain. I eventually hit a level of frustration that I had never experienced before and didn't know how to get out of it. My cry for help was for anyone or anything to come to my rescue. I just ran out of solutions for my situation.

*This is when my discovery happened.*

One night shortly after my meltdown, while sleeping soundly, the word "triune" began to softly pound in my head like a mantra. I woke up a little startled and decided to go look up the word in my favorite dictionary (this was WAY before Google.) The definition said '**triune** (try-une) – 1) a group of three things; united. 2) Being 3 in 1 such as *humans are mental, physical and spiritual.* I scratched my head, got a glass of water and went back to bed.

The next day while driving around town, I began thinking about things that I was taught in my younger years that came in threes. My Boy Scout manual taught that to have **character**, I needed to be *1) physically strong, 2) mentally awake and 3) morally straight.* My high school football coach would say emphatically "If you want to be **a good football player**, you have to be *1) mobile 2) agile and 3) hostile!*" My first sales manager shared with me that to be **a successful salesman**, I needed to have *1) sales skills, 2) product knowledge and 3) a good image.*

"Hmm", I thought, "wonder if there are other examples out there of things that work in threes?" So, some 40 years later, I have researched and discovered that many, many things work in threes. What this message was telling me is that to achieve success or balance in any significant area of my life, the three things that area consisted of had to be present continuously. That's when I had my epiphany. This discovery was telling me the secret to how life <u>really</u> works.

*Tryune is a play on the word "triune" as an invitation to "try" this concept. Furthermore, we do not say that life <u>only</u> works in threes. Life also works in ones, twos, fours and so on. What has been observed though is that the many things significant to life, just so happen to come and work in threes. That's what is being shared in this book.*

Now, you are about to see 40+ years of research and proof that life works in threes. I did not make up any of these topics. I invite you to research them on the internet to validate what is written here. There are some interesting facts that most of us have never realized...until now.

# How Life Works in Threes (around 200 examples)

## <u>LIFE</u>

**Humans consist of** *body, mind and soul.*

**A human's basic needs** are *health, income and provisions.*

**A human's basic wants** are *comfort, gain and approval.*

**Our minds are made up of** the *conscious, the subconscious and the unconscious.*

**Philosophy explains** *the id, the ego and superego.*

**Atoms** consist of *protons, neutrons and electrons.*

**Motion** is explained by *three basic laws.*

**Science** falls under three main branches: *natural, social and formal sciences*

**Time** is *past, present and future*...at the same time.

**Electricity** consists of *ohms, amperes and voltage.*

**Music's basic elements** are *duration, pitch and timbre.*

**Democracy** is a government *of the people, by the people and for the people.*

**U.S. branches of government** are *the judicial, the executive and the legislative.*

**Armed Forces** protect us on *land, air and sea.*

**Environmentally,** we are asked *to reduce, recycle and re-use.*

**The news program** gives us *the news, sports and conditions.*

**Our days** consist of *morning, afternoon and evening.*

**Three months** in each season of the year

**Our main meals** are known as *breakfast, lunch and dinner.*

**A balanced diet** consists of *good proteins, carbohydrates and fats.*

**Traditional Family consists of** *father, mother, and child(ren)*

## <u>SCIENCES</u>

**Three major branches of natural science** – *(physical, earth/ space and life sciences)*

**Three major branches of modern physics** - *(classical, relativistic, quantum)*

**Three major branches of biology** *(botany, zoology, microbiology)*

**Three spatial dimensions**: *height* (up/down), *width* (left/ right) and *depth* (forwards/backwards)

**Three-gauge bosons** (photon, gluon, W&Z bosons)

**Three types of elementary particles** *(leptons, quarks, gauge bosons)*

**Three quarks in every proton** *(two "up" and one "down")*

**Three primary colors of light** *(red, green, blue)*

**Three color tone properties** *(hue, value, chroma)*

**Three laws of motion** (*Newton's laws*)

**Three laws of planetary motion** (*Kepler's laws*)

**Three layers of the Sun's interior** (*core, radiative zone, convective zone*)

**Three layers of the Sun's atmosphere** (*photosphere, chromosphere, corona*)

**Three types of meteorites** (*iron, stony iron, stony*)

**Three types of galaxy shapes** (*elliptical, spiral, irregular*)

**Three substances of the universe** (*normal matter, 'dark matter', 'dark energy'*)

**Three phases of the moon** (*new moon, first quarter, full moon*)

**Three planetary regions** (*temperate, sub-tropical, tropical*)

**Three layers of the Earth** (*crust, mantle, core*)

**Three components of an ecosystem** (*producers, consumers, decomposers*)

**Three types of rocks** (*igneous, sedimentary, metamorphic*)

**Three types of fossil fuels** (*coal, crude oil, natural gas*)

**Three hydrological processes** (*evaporation, condensation, precipitation*)

**Three basic types of (meteorological) precipitation** (*liquid, freezing, frozen*)

**Three types of substances** *(mono-constituent, multi-constituent, UVCB)*

**Three phases of (normal) matter** *(solid, liquid, gas)*

**Three types of covalent chemical bonds** *(single, double and triple bonds)*

**Three isotopes of hydrogen** *(protium, deuterium, tritium)*

**Three atoms in each molecule of water** *(two hydrogen atoms and an oxygen atom)*

**Three endings to salts** *(-ide, -ite, -ate)*

**Three requirements for fire** *(fuel, oxygen, heat)*

**Three nucleotide bases** in a genetic codon

**Three domains of life** *(archaea, bacteria and eukaryotes)*

**Three major groups of flowering plants** *(monocots, eudicots, magnolids)*

**Three major functions that are basic to plant growth and development**: *(photosynthesis* [making sugars], *respiration* [metabolizing those sugars], and *transpiration* [water vapor loss]

**Three things that the chlorophyll in plants needs for photosynthesis to take place**: *(sunlight, carbon dioxide and water)*

**Transpiration serves three roles**: *(cooling the plant, moving minerals* and *sugars through the plant,* and *maintaining the turgidity pressure* [stiffness] *of the plant's cells)*

**Three parts of an insect's body** *(head, thorax, abdomen)*

## <u>BIOLOGY</u>

**Three types of cones in the retina**, relating to the three primary colors

**Three semi-circular canals in the ear** *(lateral, anterior, posterior)*

**Three sections in the ear** *(outer, middle, inner)*

**Three ossicles in the middle ear** *(malleus, incus, stapes)*

**Three segments to each limb** *(proximal, mid, distal)*

**Three bones in each arm** *(humerus, radius, ulna)*

**Three joints in the arm** *(shoulder, elbow, wrist)*

**Three joints in the leg** *(hip, knee, ankle)*

**Three joints in the elbow** *(humeroulnar, humeroradial, proximal radioulnar)*

**Three functional compartments in the knee joint** *(the femoropatellar, medial femorotibial* and *lateral femorotibial articulations)*

**Three types of fibrous joints** *(sutures, gomphoses, syndesmoses)*

**Three types of bone in each hand** (*carpals, metacarpals, phalanges*)

**Three types of bone in each foot** (*tarsals, metatarsals, phalanges*)

**Three bones (phalanges) in each finger and in each toe** (*proximal, intermediate, distal*)

**Three layers of skin** (*dermis, epidermis, hypodermis*)

**Three components of a cell** (*cell membrane, nucleus, cytoplasm*)

**Three types of blood vessels** (*arteries, veins, capillaries*)

**Three types of blood cells** [*red* (erythrocytes), *white* (leukocytes), *platelets* (thrombocytes)]

**Three processes of the intestinal tract** (*ingestion, digestion, excretion*)

**Three germ layers** (*Endoderm, Mesoderm, Ectoderm*)

**Three parts of a human tooth** (*crown, neck, root*)

**Three organs of otolaryngology** (*ear, nose, throat*)

**Three major body systems** (*digestive, circulatory, respiratory*)

**Three parts to a neuron:** (*soma* [*cell body*], *axon, dendrites*)

**Three main parts of the brain** (*forebrain, midbrain, hindbrain*)

**Three parts of the forebrain** *(cerebrum, thalamus, hypothalamus)*

**Three parts of the midbrain** *(colliculi, tegmentum, cerebral peduncles)*

**Three parts of the hindbrain** *(cerebellum, pons, medulla)*

**Three membranes enclosing the brain** *(dura mater, arachnoid, pia mater)*

**The brain operates on three levels:** *consciously* (for cognitive thought and declarative memory); *subconsciously* (for pre-planned actions and procedural memory); and *unconsciously* (for breathing, heart beating, etc.)

**Our conscious mind is fed from three sources**: *our senses* (which can be fooled); *our memory* (which is flawed); and *our imagination* (which is inventive)

**Three aspects of the human mind** *(memory, intellect, will)*

**Three parts of the human personality** *(id, ego, superego)*

**The sum of human capacity consists of three abilities** *(thought, word and deed)*

**Three times of man** *(birth, life, death)*

**Three periods of the Gait Cycle** *(initial double limb support, single limb support, and terminal double limb support)*

## <u>MUSIC</u>

**Three types of musical notes** *(sharps, flats, naturals)*

**Three aspects of a song** (*lyrics, melody, rhythm*)

**Three types of musical chords** (*root, third, fifth*)

## MATHEMATICS

**Three types of a real number** (*positive, negative, zero*)

**Three parts to any arithmetic operation**: for addition: *augend, addend and sum* - for subtraction: *minuend, subtrahend and difference* - for multiplication: *multiplicand, multiplier and product* - for division: *dividend, divisor and quotient*

**Three laws of arithmetic operations** (*commutative, associative, distributive*)

**Three types of equivalence relation** (*reflexivity, symmetry, transitivity*)

**Three types of symmetry operations** (*translation, rotation, reflection*)

**Three geometries** (*Euclidean, spherical, hyperbolic*)

**The number 3 is the basis of an entire branch of mathematics, called trigonometry** (from the Greek *trigonon* "triangle" + *metron* "measure")

**Three trigonometric functions** (*sine, cosine, tangent*)

**Three types of average** (*mean, mode, median*)

## GRAMMAR

**Three logical operators** (*AND, OR and NOT*)

**Three laws of logic** (*identity, noncontradiction, excluded middle*)

**Three parts of a logical syllogism** (*major premise, minor premise, conclusion*)

**Three grammatical parts to a sentence** (*subject, verb, complement*)

**Three persons in grammar** [*1st person* (I/we), *2nd* (you or your), *3rd* (he/she/it/they)]

**Three genders in grammar** [*masculine* (he/him), *feminine* (she/her), *neuter* (it)]

**Three forms of comparison in grammar** [*positive, comparative* (more, -er), *superlative* (most, -est)]

**Three cases in (English) grammar** [*subjective/nominative* (he), *objective/accusative* (him) and *possessive/genitive* (his)]

**Three parts of a narrative** (*beginning, middle, end*)

**Components of an essay** (*introduction, body, conclusion*)

**Elements of a rhetorical appeal** (*ethos, pathos, logos*)

**Aspects of a story** (*plot, characters, setting*)

## <u>RELIGION</u>

**The Creator** – *omniscient, omnipotent, omnipresent*

**Christian God** – *Father, Son, Holy Spirit*

**Jesus** – *The Way, The Truth, The Life*

**Ancient Near East**- *Qudshu, Astarte, Anat*

**Classical Antiquity** – Many dieties came in threes

**Hinduism** – Para Brahman is *Brahma, Visnu, Shiva*

**Ancient Celtic Cultures** – *many example of triad dieties*

**Buddhism** – *The three jewels*

**Taoism** – *The three pure ones*

**Islam** – *Fear, Hope and Love*

**Baha'i** - *Intention, Power and Action*

**Confucianism** – *Benevolence, Wisdom and Courage*

## <u>OTHER TRIUNE EXAMPLES</u>

**3 Coins in a Fountain**

**3 Days of the Condor**

**3 Miles in a League**

**3 Goals in a Hat Trick**

**3 Piece Suit**

**3 Feet in a Yard**

3 Books in Lord of the Rings

3 Ring Circus

3 Ships of Christopher Columbus

3 Sheets to the Wind

3 Books in a Trilogy

3 Wheels on a Tricycle

3 Wise Men

3-Legged Race

3 Ring Circus

3-Wheeler

3 Cornered Hat

3 Dimensional

3 Musketeers

3 R's (reading, 'riting, 'rithmatic)

3 Sides of a triangle

3 Races in the Triple Crown (horse racing)

3 Angles in a Triangle

3 Trimesters in a Pregnancy

3 Flavors in Neapolitan Ice Cream

3 Stars in Orion's belt

3 Barleycorns in an Inch

3 Hands on a Clock (with the Seconds Hand)

3 Colors in a Flag

3 Minute Egg

3 Great Pyramids at Giza

3 Holes in a Bowling Ball

3 Colors in a Set of Traffic Lights

3 Minutes in a Boxing Round

3 Teaspoons in a Tablespoon

3 Legs on a Stool

3 Monastic Vows (Obience, Stability, Conversatio Morum)

3 Body Types: Endomorph, Mesomorph, Ectomorph

3 Ring Notebooks

3 Germ layers: Endoderm, Mesoderm, Ectoderm

3 Species of Homo: Homo habilis, Homo erectus, Homo sapiens

3 Basic parts of a camera: Lens, Shutter, Sensor

3 Stages of a Project lifecycle: initiation, planning, execution

The Truth, The Whole Truth and Nothing but the Truth

Life, Liberty and the Pursuit of Happiness

Hear no Evil, See no Evil, Speak no Evil

National motto of France/Haiti: Liberty, Equality, Fraternity

Paper, Rock, Scissors

Ready, Aim, Fire

On Your mark, Get Set, Go

Olympic medals of gold, silver, bronze

Types of joints (ball & socket, hinge, pivot)

Stages of a rocket launch (launch, orbit, re-entry)

Parts of a joke (setup, delivery, punchline)

Primary components of a transistor (emitter, base, collector)

Primary components of an airplane (fuselage, wings, empennage)

Basic components of a computer: CPU, memory, storage

**Three phases in the development of technology** (*eotechnic* [*mechanical*], *paleotechnic* [*steam-powered*] and *neotechnic* [*electric-powered*]

**Communication systems require three components** (*transmitter, channel, receiver*)

The list goes on. See if you can find more examples as they are everywhere in our universe! Now that you know that life works in threes (with proof!), we can begin to apply this concept to whatever topics we want.

So, to overcome struggles in divorce, we need to apply the three areas that going through divorce consists of – ADJUST, HEAL and PLAN. Let's get started!

ADJUST
DIVORCE
HEAL
PLAN

# DIVORCE

In today's world, the view of divorce has shifted significantly from previous generations. While it used to be stigmatized and seen as a failure, the modern perspective acknowledges that relationships can evolve, and sometimes parting ways is the healthiest option for all involved. Society has become more understanding of the complexities of human connections and the importance of personal fulfillment. Divorce is now often viewed as a courageous decision to prioritize happiness and emotional well-being over societal expectations.

The legal and cultural frameworks surrounding divorce have adapted to reflect these changing attitudes. Laws have evolved to make divorce more accessible and less punitive, focusing instead on fair division of assets and ensuring the well-being of any children involved. There's also greater emphasis on collaborative divorce processes and mediation, aiming to reduce conflict and promote amicable separations whenever possible. This shift underscores a broader cultural move towards empathy, understanding, and support for individuals navigating the complexities of relationships.

Lastly, the portrayal of divorce in media and popular culture has played a role in shaping modern perceptions. Rather than depicting divorce as a tragedy, it's often portrayed as a transformative experience where individuals can grow, heal, and ultimately find new beginnings. This narrative shift has helped normalize divorce as a part of life's journey, rather than something to be ashamed of. As a result, more people feel empowered to make decisions that align with their own happiness and well-being, knowing they are not alone in navigating the challenges and opportunities that divorce can bring.

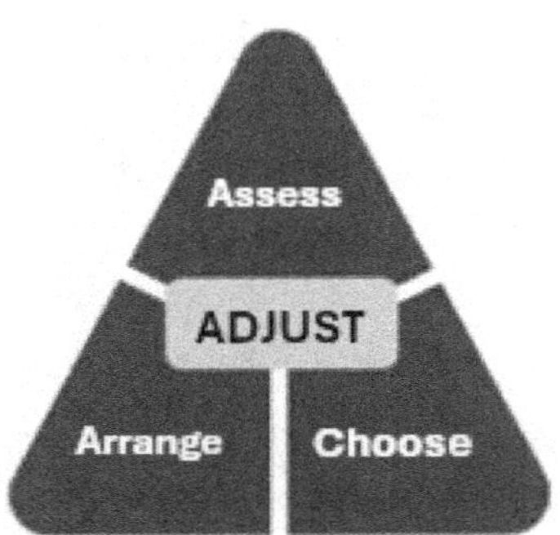

Assess
ADJUST
Arrange
Choose

# ADJUST

"We cannot direct the wind, but we can adjust our sails" is a famous quote that is apropos during post-divorce. Adjusting to life after divorce is a crucial phase that deserves patience, self-compassion, and a willingness to embrace change. It's a time to rediscover yourself, your strengths, and your passions. One of the most important aspects of this adjustment is learning to navigate new routines and responsibilities. From managing household tasks solo to restructuring your social calendar, every step forward brings opportunities for personal growth and self-discovery. Embracing this period as a chance to redefine your priorities and explore new interests can be incredibly empowering.

Equally significant is the emotional journey of healing and acceptance. Divorce often brings a mix of emotions, from relief and freedom to sadness and uncertainty about the future. It's okay to feel these emotions deeply and to give yourself permission to grieve the end of a significant chapter in your life. Seeking support from friends, family, or a therapist can provide invaluable guidance and comfort during this time. Building a strong support network and practicing self-care are essential in navigating the emotional challenges of post-divorce life with resilience and grace.

Adjusting to post-divorce life involves reevaluating your personal goals and aspirations. This is an opportunity to reflect on what truly matters to you and to set new objectives that align with your values and dreams. Whether it's pursuing a career change, traveling to new places, or focusing on personal growth, this period allows you to prioritize your own happiness and well-being. Embracing this journey with optimism and a sense of adventure can lead to unexpected opportunities and a renewed sense of purpose. Remember, adjusting to post-divorce life is not just about moving on—it's about embracing the new possibilities that lie ahead and creating a fulfilling future for yourself.

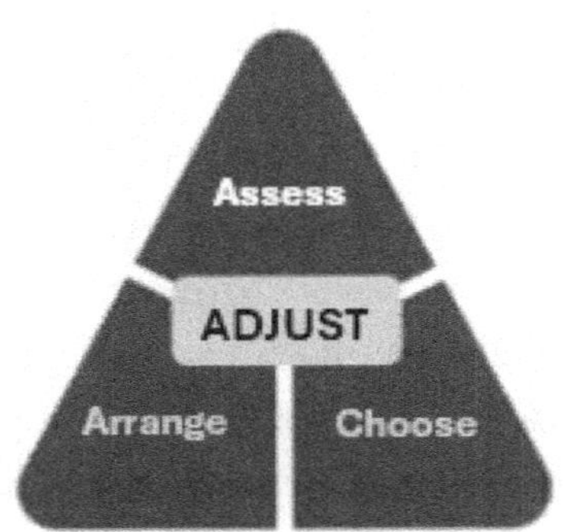
Assess
ADJUST
Arrange
Choose

# Assess

Assessing your situation during the post-divorce period is like taking stock of where you are and where you want to go next on your life's journey. It's a pivotal moment for self-reflection and introspection. By honestly evaluating your circumstances—emotionally, financially, and socially—you gain clarity on what steps to take next. This assessment isn't just about looking backward; it's about understanding your present reality so you can plan for a fulfilling future.

Emotionally, it's important to acknowledge and process the feelings that arise after a divorce. Take the time to recognize any grief, anger, or confusion you may be experiencing. Healing from the emotional wounds of divorce requires self-compassion and patience. Seek support from friends, family, or a therapist who can help you navigate these emotions with empathy and understanding. Assessing your emotional well-being allows you to gradually move forward with a clearer mind and a lighter heart.

Financially, divorce often brings significant changes to your financial situation. Assessing your new financial landscape—whether it's determining your assets, liabilities, or adjusting to a new budget—is essential for financial stability. Consider consulting with a financial advisor to help you make informed decisions about savings, investments, and long-term financial goals. Taking control of your financial future empowers you to build a secure and independent life post-divorce.

Socially, rebuilding your social circle and support network is another crucial aspect of assessing your post-divorce situation. Evaluate your relationships and identify those that are positive and supportive. Nurture these connections while also being open to new friendships and opportunities to expand your social circle. Joining clubs, community groups, or pursuing hobbies can be great ways to meet new people who share your interests and values. Building a strong social support system provides emotional resilience and a sense of belonging as you navigate this new chapter of your life.

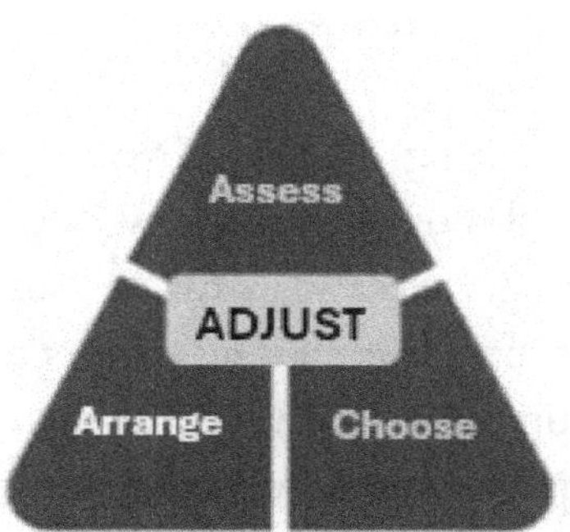
Assess
ADJUST
Arrange
Choose

# Arrange

Making arrangements during the post-divorce period is essential for establishing stability and moving forward with confidence. One of the first priorities is creating a clear plan for co-parenting if children are involved. Effective co-parenting arrangements ensure that children maintain strong relationships with both parents while minimizing conflict and confusion. This might involve creating a parenting schedule, establishing communication protocols, and agreeing on important decisions regarding the children's upbringing. Keeping the focus on the well-being of your children can help foster a positive co-parenting dynamic.

Financial arrangements also require attention to ensure both parties are financially secure after divorce. This includes dividing assets and debts fairly, determining child support or spousal support if applicable, and updating financial documents such as bank accounts, insurance policies, and wills. Consulting with a financial advisor or mediator can provide guidance on navigating these financial arrangements with fairness and clarity.

Additionally, making arrangements for your own well-being is crucial during this transitional period. Assess your living situation and consider whether you need to find a new home or make adjustments to your current one. Take time to prioritize self-care and establish routines that support your physical and emotional health. This might involve exploring new hobbies, reconnecting with friends and family, or seeking support through counseling or support groups. Making these arrangements empowers you to create a fulfilling and balanced life post-divorce, setting the stage for a positive future.

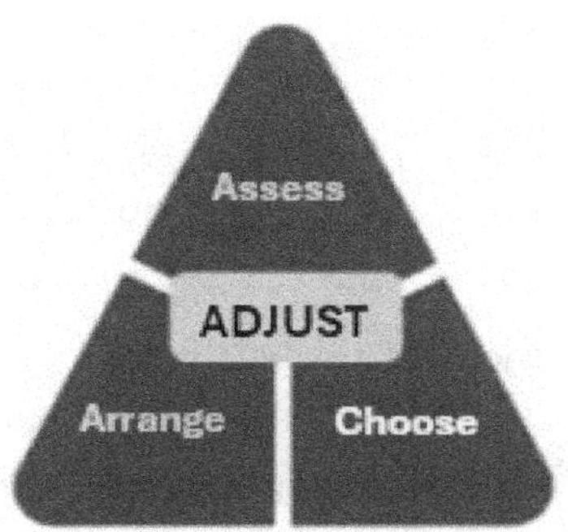
Assess
ADJUST
Arrange
Choose

# Choose

Choosing to take the "high road" during post-divorce is a powerful decision that can positively impact your well-being and the well-being of those around you. It means prioritizing respect, integrity, and compassion, even in the face of challenging emotions or difficult situations. By taking the high road, you demonstrate strength of character and a commitment to moving forward in a constructive manner. This approach can help reduce conflict, foster healthier relationships, and pave the way for a more peaceful transition into your new life.

One of the key benefits of taking the high road is preserving your own emotional health. Divorce often comes with a range of intense emotions such as hurt, anger, or disappointment. Responding with patience and understanding, rather than reacting impulsively, allows you to maintain a sense of inner peace and dignity. It also sets a positive example for others, including children if they are involved, showing them that disagreements can be handled maturely and respectfully.

Moreover, choosing the high road can lead to more amicable and effective communication with your ex-partner. Clear and respectful communication is essential, especially when co-parenting or making decisions about shared responsibilities. By focusing on solutions rather than dwelling on past grievances, you create a more cooperative environment that benefits everyone involved. This approach fosters a sense of mutual respect and facilitates smoother interactions, making it easier to navigate the practical aspects of post-divorce life.

In addition to personal benefits, taking the high road can also contribute to your long-term happiness and well-being. It allows you to let go of bitterness and resentment, freeing up mental and emotional energy to focus on your own growth and future aspirations. By choosing forgiveness and understanding, you open yourself up to new opportunities and possibilities. Ultimately, taking the high road during post-divorce is not just about handling the present situation—it's about creating a foundation for a positive and fulfilling future.

Support
HEAL
Tools
Forgiveness

# HEAL

Healing during the post-divorce process is essential for moving forward with resilience and embracing a brighter future. Divorce can leave emotional wounds that need time and care to heal. It's important to give yourself permission to feel and process your emotions—whether it's sadness, anger, relief, or a mix of everything. Healing isn't about forgetting the past but rather about finding peace and acceptance within yourself. This journey of healing allows you to rediscover your sense of self-worth and rebuild your confidence.

Self-care plays a crucial role in the healing process. Taking time to nurture your physical, emotional, and mental well-being can help you regain a sense of balance and stability. This might involve engaging in activities that bring you joy and relaxation, such as exercise, hobbies, or spending time with supportive friends and family. Prioritizing self-care isn't selfish—it's a necessary step in rebuilding your strength and resilience after the challenges of divorce.

Seeking support from others can provide valuable comfort and perspective during the healing process. Whether it's through talking to trusted friends and family members or seeking guidance from a therapist or support group, sharing your feelings and experiences with others can help you feel less alone. Surrounding yourself with positive influences and compassionate listeners can offer encouragement and validation as you navigate the ups and downs of post-divorce life. Remember, healing is a gradual process, and everyone's journey is unique. By prioritizing healing, you empower yourself to heal wounds, grow stronger, and embrace new possibilities for happiness and fulfillment in the future.

Support
HEAL
Tools
Forgiveness

# Support

Support during the post-divorce healing process is like having a safety net that helps you navigate through uncertain times with strength and resilience. Whether it's from friends, family, or a support group, having a strong support system can provide comfort, encouragement, and valuable perspective. These individuals can offer a listening ear, practical advice, or simply companionship during moments when you feel overwhelmed or unsure. Their unwavering presence reminds you that you're not alone on this journey.

Seeking professional support, such as therapy or counseling, can be incredibly beneficial. A trained therapist can help you process complex emotions, identify unhealthy patterns, and develop coping strategies for dealing with stress and anxiety. Therapy provides a safe space to explore your feelings and gain insights into yourself, facilitating healing and personal growth. It's a proactive step towards rebuilding your emotional well-being and reclaiming a sense of control over your life.

In addition to emotional support, practical assistance can also lighten your load during this transitional period. Whether it's help with childcare, household tasks, or navigating legal matters, accepting support from others allows you to focus on your own healing and adjustment. Don't hesitate to reach out and communicate your needs—friends and family often want to help but may not know how best to support you unless you ask. By building a strong support network and embracing the help offered, you create a foundation of strength and resilience that empowers you to heal and thrive after divorce.

Support
HEAL
Tools
Forgiveness

# Tools

Navigating post-divorce trauma can be emotionally challenging, and mental health tools can play a pivotal role in supporting your healing journey. One invaluable tool is therapy or counseling. A qualified therapist can provide a safe and non-judgmental space to explore your emotions, process grief, and develop coping strategies for managing stress and anxiety. Therapy helps you gain insights into patterns of behavior, build resilience, and regain a sense of control over your life. It's a proactive step towards healing emotional wounds and rebuilding your self-confidence after the upheaval of divorce.

Mindfulness and meditation techniques can be powerful tools for managing stress and promoting emotional well-being. These practices teach you to stay present in the moment, acknowledge your feelings without judgment, and cultivate inner peace. Mindfulness can help reduce the intensity of negative emotions and improve overall mental clarity and resilience. Apps and online resources offer guided meditations and mindfulness exercises that you can incorporate into your daily routine, helping to alleviate stress and foster a sense of calm amidst life's challenges.

Peer support groups can provide valuable camaraderie and solidarity during the post-divorce healing process. Connecting with others who have experienced similar challenges can offer empathy, understanding, and practical advice. Peer support groups create a sense of community where you can share your story, receive validation, and gain perspective from different viewpoints. Knowing that you're not alone in your struggles can be incredibly comforting and empowering as you navigate the emotional ups and downs of rebuilding your life post-divorce.

By embracing these mental health tools—therapy, mindfulness practices, and peer support—you equip yourself with the resources needed to heal from post-divorce trauma and cultivate emotional well-being. Each tool offers unique benefits in promoting self-awareness, resilience, and personal growth, empowering you to navigate this transitional period with strength and positivity. Remember, healing takes time, but with the right tools and support, you can emerge stronger and more resilient than ever before.

Support
HEAL
Tools
Forgiveness

# Forgiveness

Forgiveness plays a profound role in the healing process during and after divorce, offering emotional liberation and paving the way for personal growth. Firstly, forgiving your ex-partner allows you to release the negative emotions that may be holding you back, such as anger, resentment, or hurt. It's not about condoning their actions but rather about freeing yourself from the emotional burden that can hinder your own happiness and well-being. Forgiveness is a gift you give yourself, enabling you to move forward with a lighter heart and a renewed sense of inner peace.

Also, forgiveness fosters personal growth and resilience. It involves letting go of grudges and embracing empathy and understanding. By acknowledging the humanity in both you and your ex-partner, you cultivate compassion and strengthen your emotional resilience. This mindset shift empowers you to learn from the past, grow from your experiences, and approach future relationships with greater wisdom and maturity. Forgiveness opens doors to new opportunities and allows you to rebuild your life on a foundation of positivity and acceptance.

Finally, forgiveness can improve co-parenting relationships if children are involved. Letting go of bitterness and fostering a cooperative co-parenting dynamic benefits children by providing a stable and nurturing environment. It demonstrates to them that disagreements can be handled maturely and respectfully, setting a positive example for their own emotional development. Forgiveness in co-parenting helps prioritize the well-being of your children and fosters a sense of unity despite the challenges of divorce. Ultimately, forgiveness is a powerful tool that empowers you to reclaim your happiness, cultivate healthier relationships, and embrace a future filled with hope and possibility after divorce.

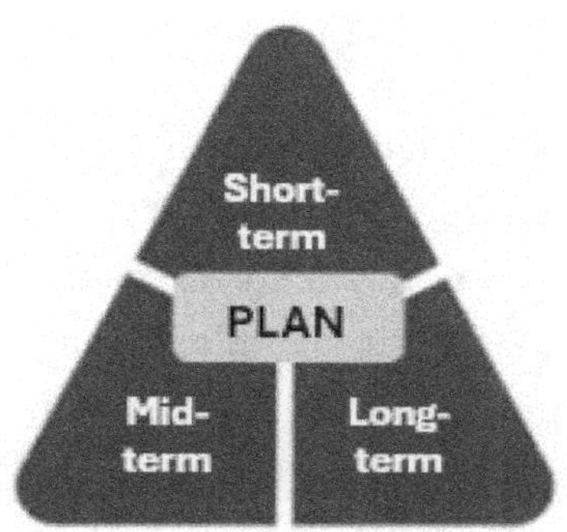

Short-
term
PLAN
Mid-
term
Long-
term

# PLAN

Having a well-thought-out plan during the post-divorce period is like having a roadmap to guide you through the transitions and uncertainties that come with starting afresh. Firstly, a practical plan helps provide a sense of direction and stability. It allows you to set clear goals for yourself—whether they're related to finances, housing, co-parenting, or personal development—and outline the steps needed to achieve them. This proactive approach empowers you to take control of your life and navigate challenges with confidence.

Secondly, a plan fosters a sense of security and preparedness. Divorce often brings significant changes to your lifestyle and responsibilities. By outlining your priorities and establishing a timeline for accomplishing tasks, you reduce uncertainty and minimize stress. This might involve creating a budget, updating legal documents, or exploring new career opportunities. Having a plan in place gives you peace of mind knowing that you're actively working towards your goals and adapting to your new circumstances effectively.

Lastly, a well-crafted plan encourages you to stay focused on the future while honoring the lessons learned from the past. It helps you identify potential obstacles and develop strategies for overcoming them. Additionally, seeking guidance from professionals, such as financial advisors or therapists, can provide valuable insights and support as you navigate this transitional period. Remember, flexibility is key—adjust your plan as needed based on new developments or changing priorities. Ultimately, having a structured plan during the post-divorce period empowers you to embrace new opportunities, rebuild your life with intention, and move forward with optimism and resilience.

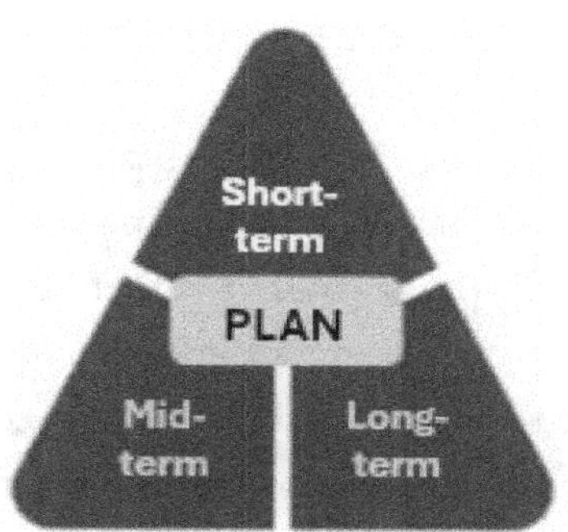
Short-
term
PLAN
Mid-
term
Long-
term

# Short-Term

Short-term planning during the post-divorce phase is crucial for managing immediate challenges and laying a solid foundation for long-term stability and happiness. Firstly, focusing on short-term goals allows you to break down larger tasks into manageable steps. Whether it's finding a new place to live, adjusting to a new co-parenting schedule, or securing employment, setting short-term objectives gives you clarity on what needs to be accomplished first. This approach helps you stay organized and motivated as you navigate through the initial adjustments following a divorce.

Secondly, short-term planning provides a sense of accomplishment and progress. Celebrating small victories, such as completing a job application, finalizing a custody arrangement, or setting up a new budget, boosts your confidence and reinforces your ability to handle challenges effectively. Each achievement contributes to rebuilding your sense of independence and self-worth, which is crucial for emotional well-being during this transitional period.

Furthermore, short-term planning allows for flexibility and adaptation to changing circumstances. Divorce often brings unexpected changes and uncertainties. By focusing on short-term goals, you can adjust your plans as needed based on new developments or emerging priorities. This adaptive approach helps you navigate through transitions with resilience and resourcefulness, ensuring that you can respond proactively to challenges and seize opportunities as they arise.

In conclusion, short-term planning in the post-divorce phase is not just about managing immediate tasks—it's about empowering yourself to regain control over your life, rebuild your confidence, and pave the way for a brighter future. By setting achievable goals, celebrating small victories, and remaining flexible in your approach, you lay a strong foundation for long-term success and happiness after divorce.

Remember, each step forward, no matter how small, brings you closer to a life filled with renewed purpose and fulfillment.

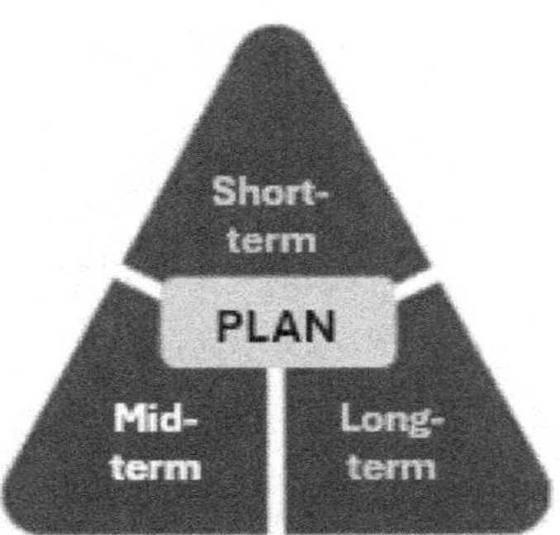
Short-
term
PLAN
Mid-
term
Long-
term

# Mid-Term

Mid-term planning during the post-divorce phase offers a strategic approach to achieving stability and building a fulfilling future. Firstly, mid-term goals typically span several months to a few years, allowing you to focus on broader objectives beyond immediate adjustments. Whether it's furthering your education, advancing your career, or saving for a major purchase, mid-term planning helps you set realistic milestones that contribute to your long-term well-being. This forward-thinking mindset enables you to envision and work towards a future that aligns with your aspirations and values.

Secondly, mid-term planning encourages you to assess and enhance your personal growth and development. This may involve prioritizing self-care, exploring new interests or hobbies, or investing in skills that enhance your professional prospects. By setting mid-term goals related to personal growth, you empower yourself to cultivate resilience and adaptability, essential qualities for navigating life's challenges with confidence and grace.

Furthermore, mid-term planning fosters a sense of purpose and direction as you rebuild your life post-divorce. It allows you to make intentional decisions about how you want to shape your future, rather than simply reacting to immediate circumstances. Whether you're focusing on improving your financial stability, strengthening relationships with loved ones, or pursuing new opportunities for personal fulfillment, mid-term planning provides a roadmap that guides you towards creating a life that reflects your values and priorities.

In conclusion, mid-term planning during the post-divorce phase is about embracing opportunities for growth, setting meaningful goals, and taking proactive steps towards a brighter tomorrow. By establishing mid-term objectives that inspire and motivate you, you cultivate resilience, build confidence, and create a sense of purpose in your journey of rebuilding after divorce. Remember, each milestone achieved brings you closer to realizing your full potential and living a life that is rich with fulfillment and happiness.

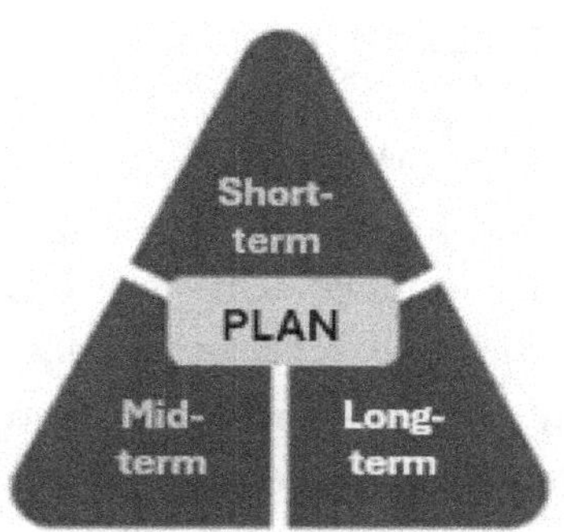
Short-
term
PLAN
Mid-
term
Long-
term

# Long-Term

During the post-divorce phase, exercising caution with long-term planning can be a wise approach as you navigate through significant life changes and emotional adjustments. Firstly, it's important to give yourself the time and space to heal emotionally. Divorce can bring a whirlwind of emotions, and rushing into long-term commitments or decisions may not align with your evolving needs and aspirations. Taking a step back allows you to process your feelings, gain clarity, and make decisions that are grounded in a more stable emotional state.

Secondly, delaying long-term plans gives you the opportunity to reassess your priorities and goals. The aftermath of divorce often requires adapting to new circumstances and redefining what success and happiness mean to you. By focusing on short and mid-term goals initially, you can experiment with different paths, explore new interests, and gain insights into what truly matters in this new chapter of your life. This exploration phase allows you to make more informed decisions about your long-term aspirations when you're ready.

Holding off on long-term plans can provide flexibility and openness to unexpected opportunities. Life after divorce can be unpredictable, and circumstances may change in ways you hadn't anticipated. By maintaining flexibility in your plans, you remain adaptable to new possibilities and can seize opportunities that align with your evolving goals and values. This approach allows for growth, exploration, and the ability to shape your future with intention and confidence when the time is right.

In conclusion, while it's important to have a vision for your future, exercising patience with long-term planning during the post-divorce phase allows you to prioritize emotional healing, reassess your priorities, and remain open to new possibilities. By taking a gradual and thoughtful approach to planning, you empower yourself to make decisions that align with your authentic self and lead to a fulfilling and purposeful life after divorce. Remember, the journey of rebuilding after divorce is unique to each individual, and embracing this process with patience and resilience can lead to transformative personal growth and happiness.

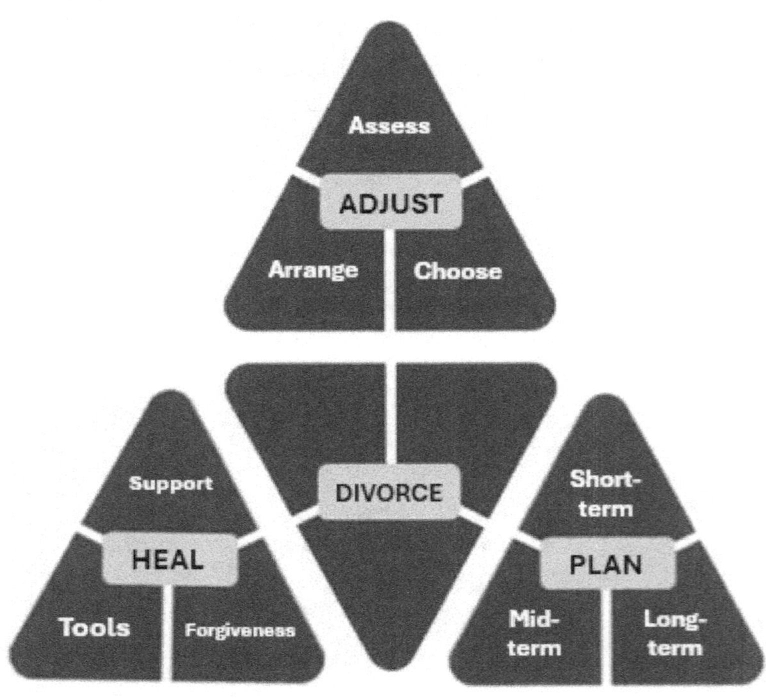
Assess
ADJUST
Arrange
Choose
Support
HEAL
Tools
Forgiveness
DIVORCE
Short-term
PLAN
Mid-term
Long-term

# SUMMARY

Despite its challenges, divorce often opens a new and transformative chapter in our lives, marked by growth, rediscovery, and personal empowerment. Firstly, it provides an opportunity for self-reflection and renewal. Going through a divorce prompts us to reassess our priorities, values, and goals, encouraging us to reconnect with our authentic selves. This process of introspection can lead to newfound clarity about what we want from life and how we envision our future, allowing us to pursue paths that align more closely with our personal aspirations.

Secondly, divorce can be a catalyst for personal growth and resilience. It challenges us to navigate through uncertainty and rebuild our lives with courage and determination. As we face the emotional upheaval and practical adjustments that come with divorce, we develop strength and resilience, learning valuable lessons about perseverance and adaptability along the way. This journey of growth empowers us to overcome obstacles, embrace change, and embrace new opportunities for happiness and fulfillment.

Thirdly, divorce opens doors to new relationships and experiences. It encourages us to explore new interests, reconnect with old passions, and forge meaningful connections with others who support and inspire us. Whether it's cultivating friendships, pursuing new hobbies, or even finding a new romantic partner, divorce can lead to enriching experiences that contribute to our personal and emotional well-being. By embracing the possibilities that divorce presents, we can embark on a journey of self-discovery and renewal, ultimately shaping a future that is filled with hope, resilience, and a renewed sense of purpose.

# Invitation

I'm going to share something that I learned while going through a divorce that actually proved itself to be true. After 23 years of marriage, it was time to part ways and the divorce process happened quickly, but the healing process took much longer than I anticipated. In my situation, I took a double whammy with a divorce and empty nest at the same time. Fortunately, I gave in to visiting a therapist to help me through this process.

My therapist gave me some helpful tools to use during this process but the one thing that really hit home with me was his suggestion on how much time is needed to heal. He knew this because he had counseled many people going through the same thing. Here's what he said, "For every year you were married, take that many months to heal before getting involved in another relationship. For example, in your case, you were married 23 years...so take 23 months to heal properly."

Naturally, I ignored his advice and got involved with someone as I was lonely and wanted desperately to replace the partner that I had with another. I was not used to being alone ever in my life. Suffice it to say that my decision didn't work. I surrendered and took the advice of 23 months and guess what? It worked. I needed the time to look within myself and think about how I could become a better partner in the future. I worked on improving myself in several areas and got re-energized to put myself back out there in a healed state.

My invitation is to maybe try doing the same thing for yourself. Give yourself time to heal by taking a month for every year you were married. Rushing into another relationship (some call it "rebound") to fill a hole in your life doesn't give you time to give yourself fully to someone else. And that's not fair to the other person. It won't be easy, but it will be helpful in the long run. Unraveling relationships are some of the toughest things we go through in life. Give it time.

*When you're with someone who is sharing their struggles with you...just smile at him/her and give them one of these. He/she will ask "What is that?" Then simply reply "Life Works in Threes."*

# Other titles coming out:

- Weight Struggles?
- Abundance Struggles?
- Parenting Struggles?
- Life Struggles?
- Purpose Struggles?
- Happiness Struggles?
- Sales Struggles?
- Speaker Struggles?
- Time Struggles?
- Network Struggles?
- Marriage Struggles?
- Romance Struggles?
- Money Struggles?
- Career Struggles?
- Dating Struggles?
- Caretaker Struggles?
- Forgiveness Struggles?
- Grieving Struggles?
- Success Struggles?
- Golf Struggles?
- Workplace Struggles?
- Stress Struggles?
- Shame/Guilt Struggles?
- Addiction Struggles?

*Remember,*
*When you get right down to it,*

*Life is about making choices.*

*Every day, all day long, that's what we do.*

- *We choose to get out of bed or not.*
- *We choose to clean up or not.*
- *We choose what to eat all day.*
- *We choose to exercise or not.*
- *We choose to go to work or not.*
- *We choose to do a good job or not.*
- *We choose to come home or not.*
- *We choose to watch TV or do something constructive.*
- *We choose to bed at a decent hour or not.*

*And the next day...we start all over again.*

*What is the meaning of this? Get good at choosing.*

*Before you can get good at choosing though...you need to understand how life works in threes.*

# Quotes about Divorce

"Divorce isn't such a tragedy. A tragedy is staying in an unhappy marriage, teaching your children the wrong things about love." - Jennifer Weiner

"Divorce isn't the child's fault. Don't say anything unkind about your ex to the child, because you're really just hurting the child." - Valerie Bertinelli

"Divorce is like an amputation. You survive it, but there's less of you." - Margaret Atwood

"Divorce is a declaration of defeat, but in the end you wear it as a badge of honor because you survived it." - Daphne Zuniga

"Divorce isn't the end of the world. It's the end of a bad relationship." - Unknown

I remember when I went through my divorce, loneliness was a real problem. My normal routine for years was suddenly disrupted, and I became disoriented during the process. Here are several suggestions for divorced individuals to help avoid loneliness:

1.  **Engage in Hobbies and Interests:** Rediscover or develop hobbies that bring joy and fulfillment.
2.  **Socialize:** Make an effort to connect with friends, family, or colleagues regularly.
3.  **Join Clubs or Groups:** Participate in clubs, organizations, or meetups that align with your interests.
4.  **Volunteer:** Contribute to the community and meet like-minded people through volunteering.
5.  **Take Classes:** Enroll in courses or workshops to learn something new and meet new people.
6.  **Exercise:** Physical activity not only boosts mood but can also provide opportunities to socialize (e.g., group classes, sports).
7.  **Travel:** Explore new places and cultures, either solo or with friends.
8.  **Attend Events:** Concerts, exhibitions, lectures, and other events can be great places to meet people with similar interests.
9.  **Therapy or Support Groups:** Seek professional support or join support groups to share experiences and receive emotional support.
10. **Pets:** Consider adopting a pet for companionship and to help establish routine and responsibility.
11. **Mindfulness and Self-Care:** Practice mindfulness, meditation, or other self-care activities to promote

well-being.

12. **Develop Goals:** Set personal goals and work towards them; achieving goals can boost confidence and self-esteem.

13. **Explore Online Communities:** Join online forums or social media groups to connect with others who share similar experiences.

14. **Read and Learn:** Engage in reading or educational pursuits that stimulate the mind and provide intellectual fulfillment.

15. **Seek Professional Help:** If feelings of loneliness persist or become overwhelming, consider speaking with a therapist or counselor for additional support and guidance.

By actively pursuing these activities and strategies, divorced individuals can reduce feelings of loneliness and cultivate a fulfilling life post-divorce.

Legend has it that when going through a divorce, a person should take one month for every year they were married...to heal.

So, if you were married for 20 years, then it is wise to not get involved with another serious relationship for the next 20 months. 10 years would be 10 months, 5 years would be 5 months and so on.

The reason for this is to avoid the "rebound" stage. Newly divorced people are tempted to "hurry up" and find someone else to fill the hole their previous partner left.

I can tell you from firsthand experience that both of these statements were true for me.

It is always a good idea to visit a therapist and get his/her view on this as well.

**When someone is struggling with a particular area or two, chances are they are "out of balance" with how life works. How does life work? Life works in threes.**

If you're interested in personal topics like life, health, money or business topics like sales, time management and public speaking...TRYUNE WORKS! can shed some light on creating success in those areas.

The definition of TRIUNE is a group of three things; united. Being three in one, such as - humans are *mental, physical* and *spiritual beings*. The word TRYUNE is a play of the word TRIUNE, encouraging all to try this concept and help eliminate struggling unnecessarily.

LifeWorksInThrees.com